Hat-M

Written by
Sylvia Baxter

Photographs by
John Paul Endress

On Friday, I went to visit my friend
Margo. She is a hat maker. I wanted to
learn how to make a hat, and Margo
was going to show me.

First, Margo asked me to choose the colours of wool that I would like for my hat. She gave me a big round ball and told me to cover it all over with sticky soap.

Next, we wrapped the coloured wool all around the ball. The soap made the wool stick.

Then, we put the ball into a bag made
of material that stretched. We wet the
bag and added extra soap.

Next, we had to bounce the bagged ball
for about ten minutes. Margo explained
this helped the wool to stick together.
Then, we took the ball out of the bag.
We had a hat, but it was inside out!

We turned the hat the right way out,
and rinsed it in clean water to wash the
soap out. While the hat was still wet,
we pulled it into shape.

Finally, my hat was finished. I tried it on.
It fit perfectly! When I grow up, I think
I'll be a hat maker like Margo.